The Heart
and Circulation

Carol Ballard

FRANKLIN WATTS
LONDON•SYDNEY

First published in 2005 by
Franklin Watts
96 Leonard Street
London EC2A 4XD

Franklin Watts Australia
Level 17/207 Kent Street
Sydney NSW 2000

Produced by Arcturus Publishing Ltd,
26/27 Bickels Yard, 151–153 Bermondsey Street, London SE1 3HA

Series concept: Alex Woolf
Editor: Alex Woolf
Designer: Peta Morey
Artwork: Michael Courtney
Picture researcher: Glass Onion Pictures
Consultant: Dr Kristina Routh

Picture Credits
Science Photo Library: 5 (Scott Camazine, Sue Trainor), 7 (Zephyr),
11 (Mauro Fermariello), 13 (Susan Kuklin), 15 (Ouellette & Theroux, Publiphoto
Diffusion), 16 (Martin Riedl), 17 (Zephyr), 18 (Zephyr), 19 (James King-Holmes),
21 (Mark Clarke), 22 (David Scharf), 24 (Antonia Reeve), 25 (Sam Ogden),
26 (Antonia Reeve), 27 (Tek Image), 28 (Dr Gopal Murti), 29 (Alex Bartel).

Every attempt has been made to clear copyright. Should there be any
inadvertent omission, please apply to the publisher for rectification.

A CIP catalogue record for this book is available from the British Library

ISBN 0 7496 5964 5

Printed in Singapore

Contents

Introduction

Your heart is one of the most important organs in your body. It beats continuously every minute of every day of your life, whether you are awake or asleep, sitting still or running around. You never have to think about making your heart beat – it just does it automatically.

Your heart is inside your chest, protected by the bones of the ribcage and surrounded and cushioned by the lungs. A network of tubes called blood vessels links the heart to the lungs. Another network of blood vessels connects the heart to the rest of the body.

Your heart is a strong pump made of muscle. Every time it beats, it pushes blood around your body. Blood cannot move randomly around inside the body. Instead, it travels through blood vessels. In the same way that there are different types of road such as motorways, main roads, side roads and country lanes, there are also different types of blood vessel. Blood flows through the blood vessels in a one–way system, always moving along in the same direction.

The heart pushes blood along the networks of blood vessels, forcing it

This picture shows the position of the heart in the body.

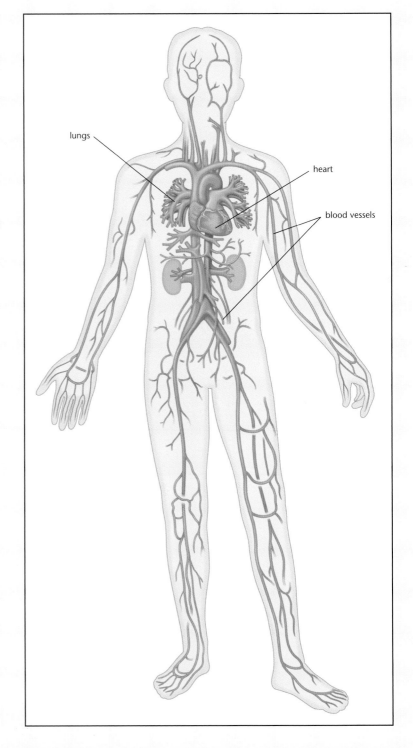

lungs

heart

blood vessels

around your body and eventually back to the heart again. Your blood travels around ... and around ... and around continuously, in a never-ending journey that is called blood circulation.

Sometimes your heart beats more quickly or more slowly than at other times. This is linked to how hard the rest of your body is working.

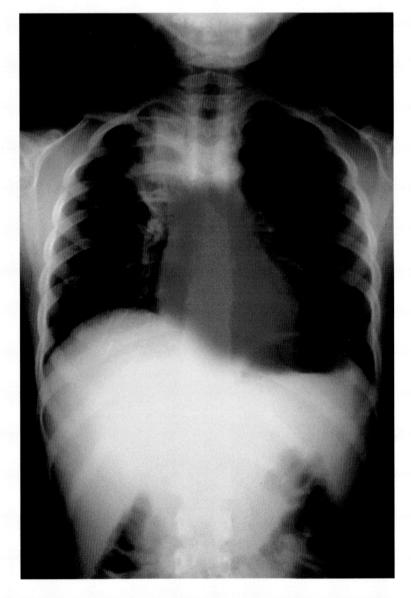

This X-ray shows the heart and lungs surrounded by the ribcage.

Like any other muscle, the heart needs to be strong to work well. This means that it needs regular exercise and a healthy diet. It is also important to avoid doing things that may damage your heart.

Blood Circulation

Blood has to reach every part of your body in order to carry out its functions of transport, control and defence. It flows around your body through a network of tubes called blood vessels.

There are two networks of blood vessels. One carries blood from the right side of your heart to your lungs.

As you breathe in, your lungs fill up with air. Oxygen from the air moves into the blood. The blood, now with lots of oxygen in it, travels back to the left side of your heart for distribution to the rest of the body.

A waste gas called carbon dioxide, which is produced by other organs and muscles, moves out of the blood into the lungs. It leaves your body when you breathe out.

The other network of blood vessels carries blood from the left side of your heart to the rest of your body. As it passes through your organs and muscles, blood supplies them with oxygen. Your blood also collects waste carbon dioxide produced by organs and muscles. Blood travels back along the blood vessels to the right side of the heart, then to the lungs, then to the left side of the heart, then to the organs and muscles, then to the right side of the heart, and on and on in a continuous journey!

Blood flows around the body in two networks of blood vessels. This diagram has been drawn as though you are looking in a mirror.

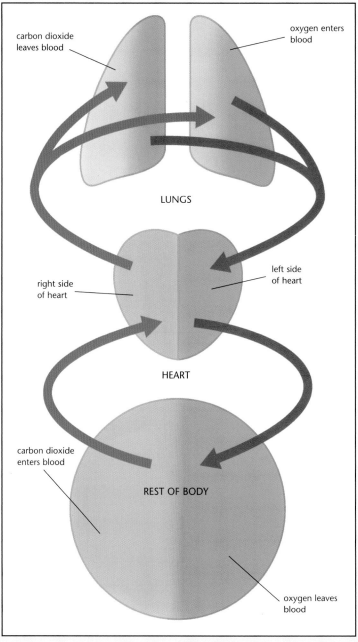

carbon dioxide leaves blood

oxygen enters blood

LUNGS

right side of heart

left side of heart

HEART

carbon dioxide enters blood

REST OF BODY

oxygen leaves blood

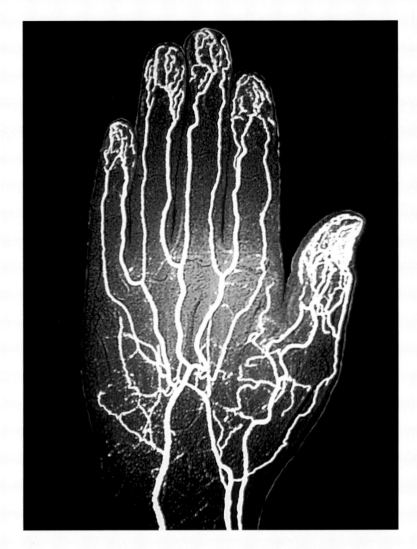

This X-ray shows some of the blood vessels in a hand.

Blood travels through blood vessels to every living part of your body, even to the very tips of your fingers and toes. Blood does not just carry oxygen and carbon dioxide, though – it carries other things too. Nutrients from your food are absorbed from your digestive system and taken to organs and muscles that need them. Waste chemicals and excess water are collected and taken away. These are removed from the blood by the liver and kidneys.

As it circulates, your blood also helps to keep your body free from germs and anything else that may cause you to be ill. Whenever you are awake or asleep, active or resting, this amazing network helps to make sure that every part of your body has everything it needs to keep it working properly.

Case notes

How many blood vessels are in my body?

There are blood vessels in every living part of your body. If you took an average adult's blood vessels and laid them all out in a straight line, they would stretch nearly 100,000 kilometres – that's long enough to go twice round the earth and still have some left over!

The Heart

Your heart is a strong, muscular organ. It contracts and relaxes to pump blood around your body. It beats continuously, without your having to think about it or control it.

Your heart is roughly the same size and shape as your fist, but with a flattened top and a slightly pointed bottom. It is tipped a little to one side, with the bottom pointing towards your left.

Just like every other muscle in your body, your heart needs a constant supply of oxygen and nutrients. Waste products made by the heart muscle also have to be removed. To do this, your heart has its own special blood vessels carrying oxygen to it and carrying away its waste. These are called the coronary arteries and veins. They form a network around the outside of the heart, so that blood can reach every part of it.

Other large blood vessels lead into and out of the heart. The pulmonary veins carry blood from the heart to the lungs and the pulmonary arteries carry blood from the lungs back to the heart. The aorta carries blood from the heart to the body and the venae cavae carry blood from the body back to the heart.

Here you can see the heart and its blood vessels.

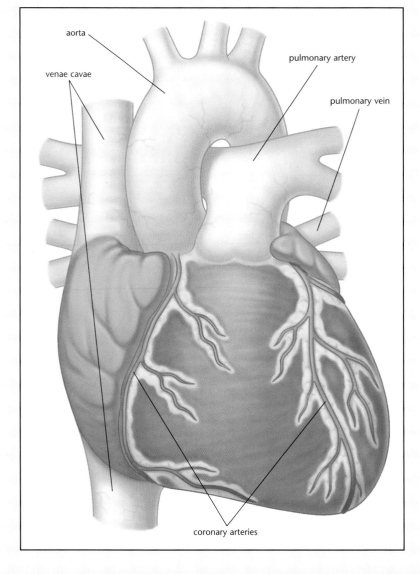

aorta

venae cavae

pulmonary artery

pulmonary vein

coronary arteries

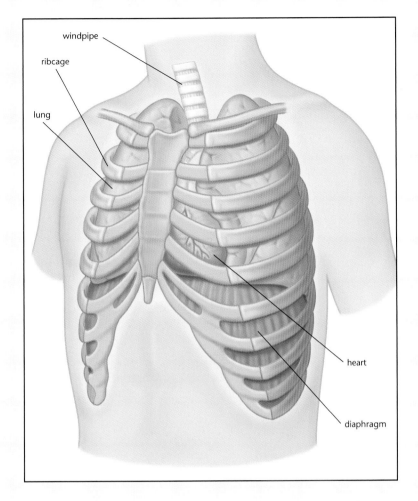

The heart lies inside the chest, protected by the bones of the ribcage.

The muscle that makes up your heart is called cardiac muscle. Although it is similar to the muscles in your arms and legs, there are some important differences. One of these is that if you damage a muscle in your arm or leg, it will heal and new muscle tissue will be made (although the muscle may not be as strong as it was before.) If cardiac muscle is damaged, only scar tissue is made. Another difference is that cardiac muscle is partly in control of when it contracts, but other muscles can only contract in response to a signal from the brain.

The heart itself has an outer layer called the pericardium, which protects the heart. This is anchored to the diaphragm below and the breastbone in front by strong fibres, so your heart is held firmly in place. The pericardium also produces a fluid that lubricates the heart so that it can move freely as it beats.

Case notes

How big is my heart?

Your heart has a mass of about two hundred grams – roughly the same as a large potato. Your heart grows along with the rest of your body, so an adult's heart is bigger and heavier than a child's.

Inside the Heart

Your heart is a pump made from strong, muscular walls with four spaces inside. These spaces are called chambers. A strong wall called the septum separates the chambers on the right from those on the left. This prevents blood in the left side from mixing with blood in the right side. The heart really operates as two separate pumps – one on each side. The right side pumps blood to the lungs. The left side pumps blood to the rest of the body. The upper chambers on each side are called atria (one is an atrium) and the lower chambers are called ventricles.

Blood flows through the heart in a one-way system. This is controlled by strong flaps called valves. These open to let blood flow through them. They then snap shut to stop the blood flowing back. The system is rather like a set of doors: one opens to let people into a room, then shuts when the room is full; another opens at the other end of the room to let people out; when the room is empty, the first one opens again to let more people in – and so on. This makes sure that the heart always has exactly the right amount of blood and can work efficiently.

This diagram shows the internal structure of the heart.

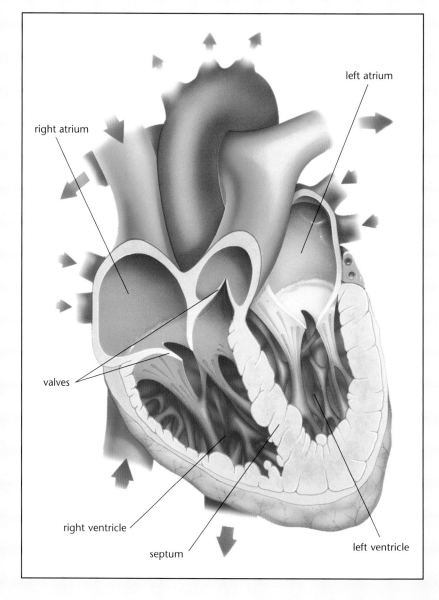

right atrium

left atrium

valves

right ventricle

septum

left ventricle

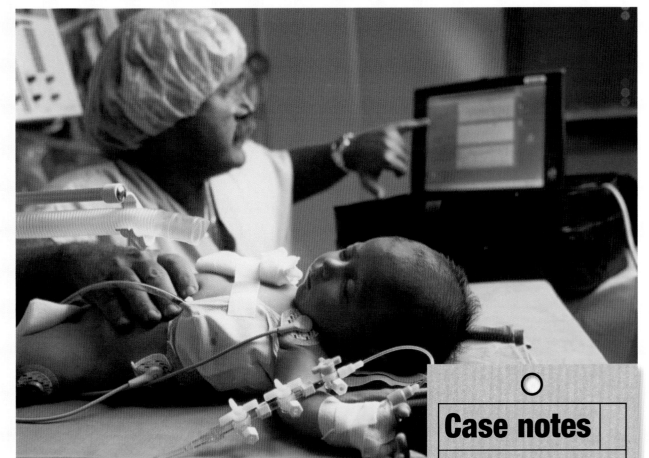

This baby is being monitored after heart surgery.

In some people, the valves do not close properly. They may have been faulty at birth, or damaged later by an illness. This means that some blood can flow backwards into the heart, so it works less efficiently. As the blood flows backwards it makes a gurgling sound that helps doctors to identify exactly what is wrong. Doctors can replace damaged or faulty valves. The first replacement valves were from animals such as pigs, but now scientists have designed artificial valves made of metal or plastic. New valves can help the heart to work properly again.

Case notes

What is a "hole in the heart"?

The septum separates the right side of the heart from the left side of the heart. This stops blood moving straight across from one side to the other. In some babies, this wall does not form properly, so there is a small gap between the two sides. This is a "hole in the heart". Blood can spill through, making the whole system less efficient, and making the baby very ill. Doctors can operate to close the hole and make the baby well again.

Heartbeat

Every time your heart beats, it pushes blood through your blood vessels. Imagine a squeezy bottle filled with liquid, with a single tube attached to either end of the bottle. The bottle stands for your heart, the tube stands for your blood vessels, and the liquid stands for your blood. If you squeeze the bottle, the liquid will be forced out of the bottle, along the tube and back into the other end of the bottle. This is just how your heart works: it squeezes to force blood out of the heart, through the blood vessels and back to the heart again.

The heartbeat sounds that you hear are made by the valves as they snap shut. There are two sounds to each heartbeat – lub-dup ... lub-dup ... lub-dup – as the two pairs of valves shut one after the other.

Each heartbeat has four stages:

1. The atria fill with blood.
2. The atria contract, pushing the blood against the valves. This forces the valves open, allowing blood to rush into the ventricles.
3. When the ventricles are full they contract and the valves between the atria and ventricles close to stop blood flowing backwards. (This makes the first "lub" sound of the heartbeat.) Instead the blood is pushed against the next set of valves. The valves

This diagram shows the steps that take place in a single heartbeat.

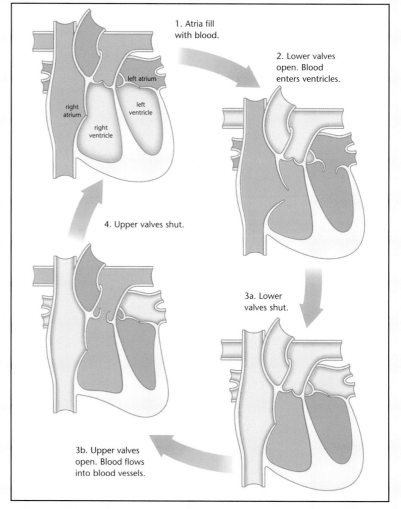

1. Atria fill with blood.

2. Lower valves open. Blood enters ventricles.

left atrium

right atrium

left ventricle

right ventricle

4. Upper valves shut.

3a. Lower valves shut.

3b. Upper valves open. Blood flows into blood vessels.

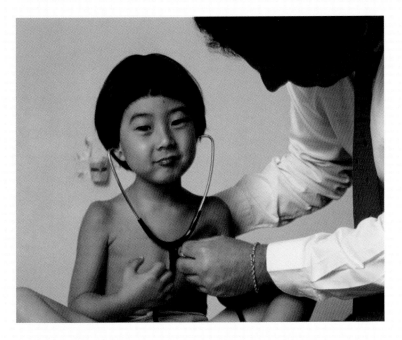

A stethoscope allows you to hear the sound of your heartbeat more clearly.

are forced open and blood is pushed out into the blood vessels.

4. The second set of valves shut, stopping the blood flowing back into the ventricles. This makes the second "dup" sound of the heartbeat.

The whole sequence happens continuously, with the atria immediately filling with blood again as soon as the ventricles empty. Each heartbeat pumps about 70 millilitres of blood.

The walls of the ventricles are thicker and stronger than those of the atria. This is because only a gentle push is needed to pump blood from the atria into the ventricles. A much stronger push is needed to pump blood out of the ventricles and into the blood vessels.

Doctors often use an instrument called a stethoscope to listen to a patient's heart. This amplifies the sound of the heartbeat, making it easier for them to hear how well the heart is working. If they want more detailed information, they may use an electrocardiograph (ECG) machine. This detects and records electrical signals from the heart as it is beating. The results can be printed onto a chart or displayed on a screen.

Case notes

How can I feel my heart beat?

If you put your hand on the left side of your chest you may be able to feel your heart beating. You can also feel it by finding your pulse. Lay the index and middle finger of one hand gently on your other wrist, in a straight line with your thumb. You might be able to feel a beat. This is called your pulse. It is caused by the heart pumping blood along the arteries.

Exercise and Heart Rate

An adult's heart usually beats between seventy and eighty times every minute when the person is resting. Some people's hearts beat more quickly than this and others beat more slowly. Most children have a faster heartbeat than this.

Your heart beats all the time. If it beats seventy times a minute, that's more than four thousand beats an hour ... more than 100,000 beats a day ... more than 35,000,000 beats a year! And that's just if you spend the whole year resting – if you run and exercise, it will be even more!

When you start to exercise, your heart starts to beat more quickly. This is because, when they work hard, your muscles need more oxygen and more energy than when

This graph shows how people's heart rates speed up when they exercise and slowly go back to their normal speeds when they rest again.

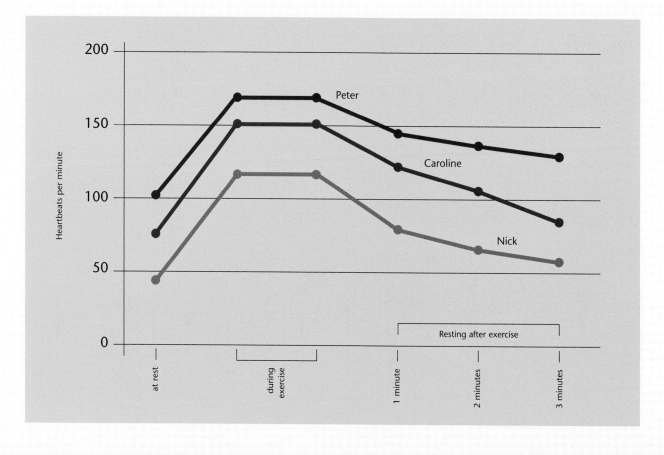

These athletes exercise regularly so their hearts are fit and strong.

they are resting. They also produce waste more quickly, which needs to be removed. Your blood carries oxygen and nutrients to the muscles, and carries away waste products. To speed up the system, your heart has to pump faster.

When you stop exercising, your muscles need less oxygen and energy, and they make a smaller amount of waste. The blood has less to do, so it does not need to be pumped as quickly. Your heart gradually slows down and goes back to its normal resting rate.

Exercise makes your heart muscle stronger, which means that it works more efficiently. It can pump more blood with each beat, so it does not need to increase its rate very much when you exercise. It also goes back to normal quickly when you stop exercising. Sportspeople who train and keep fit often have a much slower resting heart rate than people who do little exercise.

Your heart rate also speeds up if you get very excited or scared. Your body produces a special chemical that makes your heart beat more quickly. This is to keep you safe – if you were suddenly in danger and had to run away, your muscles would already have an extra supply of oxygen and energy.

Case notes

How are heart rate and breathing rate linked?

When you breathe in, oxygen passes from your lungs into your blood. Waste carbon dioxide moves out of your blood into your lungs and leaves your body when you breathe out. When you exercise, your muscles need more oxygen, so you need to breathe more quickly and deeply. Your heart then pumps more quickly to get the oxygen to your muscles. When you rest you need less oxygen, so the whole system slows down again.

Healthy Heart

Your heart is a very important organ and so it makes good sense to look after it as well as you can. There are several things you can do to keep your heart fit and healthy.

Exercise is good for your heart, just as it is for every other muscle in your body. Taking part in some regular exercise or sporting activity makes your heart fitter and stronger. Dancing, swimming, cycling, team games, gymnastics, horse riding – activities like these are all good for your heart. Many doctors recommend that you take part in some sporting or exercise activity at least four or five times a week.

Exercise like this is really good for your heart.

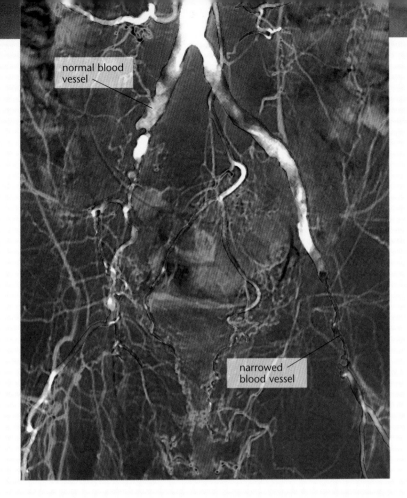

normal blood vessel

narrowed blood vessel

This X-ray shows damaged blood vessels. Blood cannot travel easily through the narrowed sections.

The food that you eat has a big effect on all of your body. Eating a balanced diet will help to keep your body, including your heart, healthy. It will also provide plenty of energy to allow you to enjoy your sporting activities. It is a good idea to try to eat something from each of these groups of foods every day:

● fresh fruit and vegetables – for vitamins and minerals
● wholemeal bread, pasta, rice or other cereals – for energy
● meats, fish, eggs and nuts – for protein

Sweet, sugary foods and fatty foods can taste great but they are not very good for your body. Try to think of these as treats – enjoy them now and again but try to avoid eating too much of this type of food.

Smoking cigarettes is really bad for your heart. Some of the chemicals in cigarette smoke can make your blood vessels narrower so your heart has to work extra hard to push the blood through them. This puts an extra strain on the heart and can lead to serious damage and heart disease.

Case notes

Does being overweight affect my heart?

Your heart has to pump blood all around your body. Being very overweight can make this more difficult. The pressure of blood in the blood vessels often increases, so every time your heart beats it has to give a harder push. Also, the heart has to pump blood to all the extra fat tissue in the body. Overall, being very overweight puts an extra strain on your heart, making it harder for it to work properly and eventually damaging it.

Heart Attacks

Every part of the body needs the constant supply of oxygen, energy and nutrients that is brought by the blood. It also needs the blood to carry away its waste products.

A heart attack is most often caused by a blockage in the coronary blood vessels. This prevents blood from reaching part of the heart muscle. Without fresh blood, this part of the heart dies. This affects the whole heart and stops it from beating properly. Without medical treatment, the patient may die.

In men, the first sign of a heart attack is often a severe chest pain. Women often have no chest pain, but feel sick and very tired. The patient's left hand and arm often tingle too, and they may find it hard to breathe. The sooner the patient receives treatment, the better their chances of making a full recovery. By giving the patient the right medicine as soon as possible, medical teams can relieve the pain and stop any more damage to the heart. Medicines can often help to remove the blockage in the coronary vessels.

If the heart has completely stopped beating, or is just twitching instead of beating normally, defibrillation equipment can be used. This gives the heart an electric shock and can make it start to beat properly again. Mouth to mouth resuscitation and chest massage may help to keep blood flowing through the body until the heart starts beating again.

After a heart attack, a patient usually needs to spend some time recovering in hospital. Doctors will usually carry

A scan like this helps doctors to monitor a heart following a heart attack.

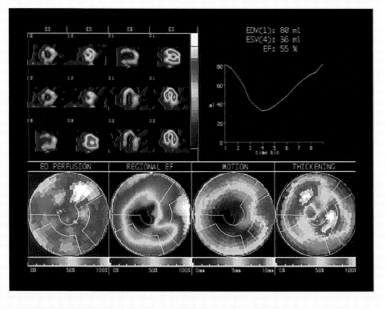

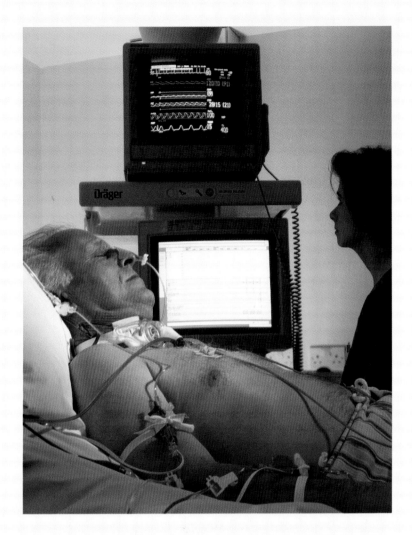

This heart-attack patient is recovering in hospital.

out tests to see how badly damaged the heart is. This will help them to decide what treatment is best for the patient.

An operation to improve the coronary blood flow may be necessary. Patients are also advised to think carefully about their lifestyle and told to try to avoid increasing the risk of another heart attack. This usually means eating a healthy, low-fat diet, taking plenty of exercise and not smoking cigarettes.

The risk of having a heart attack is highest for people who smoke cigarettes, are very overweight, take little exercise, eat fatty diets or have very stressful lives. Some diseases, such as diabetes, can increase the risk of a heart attack. Doctors also think that a person's genes may be involved too, as heart attacks seem to be more common in some families than in others.

Case notes

What should I do in an emergency?

If you are alone with someone who you think may be having a heart attack, the most important thing is not to panic. If there is an adult nearby who you think you can trust, ask him or her for help. If not, find a telephone and dial 999 for the emergency services. Tell them who you are and what the problem is. Listen carefully, answer any questions they ask you and then follow their instructions.

Blood Vessels

Blood vessels are the tubes through which blood travels to the rest of your body. Different blood vessels do different jobs, so they have different structures. There are three main types of blood vessel: arteries, veins and capillaries.

Arteries These carry blood away from the heart. Every time the heart beats, blood is forced out into the arteries under high pressure. Arteries have strong, muscular walls so that they can stand up to this pressure. The artery walls are made up of a thick outer layer, a middle layer of muscles and fibres, and a thin lining layer. The walls are flexible and stretchy.

Veins These carry blood back to the heart. The blood is under less pressure than it is in the arteries, so the walls of the veins do not need to be as strong as artery walls. The outer and inner layers of the vein walls are like those of arteries, but the middle layer is thinner and has fewer muscles.

Veins have a special valve system to stop blood flowing backwards. As blood moves towards the heart, it pushes the valves open. If blood starts to flow away from the heart, it pushes the valves shut.

Capillaries To make a complete network, arteries and veins must be linked together. Arteries branch into narrower tubes. These branch again and again, getting

These diagrams show the inner structures of arteries, veins and capillaries.

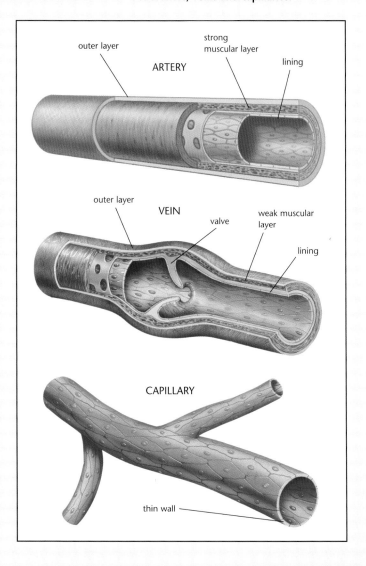

ARTERY — outer layer, strong muscular layer, lining

VEIN — outer layer, valve, weak muscular layer, lining

CAPILLARY — thin wall

narrower every time. Eventually they branch into the narrowest blood vessels, the capillaries. The capillaries carry blood through the tissues of the body and then join together again, making larger blood vessels. These join again and again, eventually making veins.

Capillaries form very fine networks throughout the body. The walls of capillaries are so thin that gases and chemicals can move through them. This means that nutrients and oxygen can move out of the blood in the capillaries and into the body tissues where they are needed. Carbon dioxide and other waste products can move out of the body tissues and into the capillaries and be carried away by the blood.

Some capillaries lie very close to the surface of your skin. When you are hot, lots of blood flows through these capillaries. This helps you to lose heat through your skin. The blood flowing close to the surface makes your skin look red. When you are cold, the opposite happens. Less blood flows through the skin capillaries, so less heat is lost and your skin looks pale.

Blood flowing through the skin capillaries makes this child's face look red, and helps him to cool down.

Case notes

What are varicose veins?

Varicose veins often look like dark, knobbly lines under the skin and are most common in the legs. People who have jobs that involve a lot of standing often get varicose veins. Pregnant women also frequently suffer from varicose veins. They occur when valves in the veins become weak. Blood flows backwards, stretching and twisting the veins. Sometimes wearing elastic stockings can help, but in more serious cases an operation may be needed.

Blood

Blood is your body's internal transport system and it defends your body against germs. It helps to control the amounts of water and chemicals in your body, and also helps to control your body's temperature. A single drop of blood contains millions and millions of tiny cells in a clear, watery liquid.

These red blood cells have been photographed under a microscope.

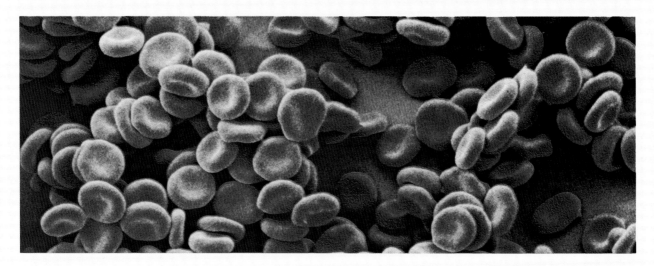

Red blood cells are like discs that have been squashed at the top and bottom. They are tiny – you would need about 125 side by side to make a line one millimetre long! Red blood cells carry oxygen around your body. It is their colour that makes your blood look red.

White blood cells can be all sorts of different shapes and sizes. They are your body's defence system. Some release special chemicals to destroy germs like bacteria and viruses. Some surround any particles that should not be in your body and destroy them. Some develop a chemical "memory" of germs so that they can attack them quickly the next time they find them.

Platelets are very, very tiny fragments of cells. They help your blood to clot and form a scab.

Plasma is the clear, watery liquid that all your blood cells float around in. It contains many different chemicals and nutrients that it carries to every part of your body. Waste chemicals are also carried in the plasma until they are removed by the liver or kidneys.

Blood cells are made in your bone marrow, the soft material at the centre of some bones. Some travel to other parts of your body to finish developing. Some white blood cells only live for a day or two. Others may live for two or three months, while a very few may live for over a year. Red blood cells live for about three months. At the end of their life, blood cells are destroyed by your spleen and liver. Some of the chemicals they were made from are stored or reused, while others leave the body in your urine.

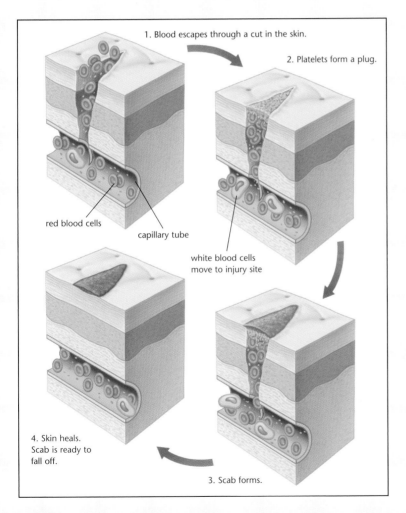

1. Blood escapes through a cut in the skin.

2. Platelets form a plug.

red blood cells

capillary tube

white blood cells move to injury site

4. Skin heals. Scab is ready to fall off.

3. Scab forms.

Platelets help a scab to form over a cut.

Blood Groups

Although all humans are alike in many ways, we are also different in other ways. For example, although we have two arms, a head and ten toes, you may be tall or short, have black hair or blonde hair, brown eyes or blue eyes. In the same way, we all have red blood cells but they may have different chemicals on their surfaces. Using these red blood cell differences, scientists put blood into different groups.

The main blood group system is called ABO. This was worked out in 1930 by Karl Landsteiner, an American scientist. The name comes from two special chemicals, A and B, that may be on your red blood cells. These chemicals determine your ABO blood group. The table shows how this works:

A technician carries out a test on some donated blood to see which group it belongs to.

Blood group	Chemical on blood cells
A	A
B	B
AB	A and B
O	neither A nor B

If blood from different groups is mixed together, they can react against each other. This would make you very ill.

Most of the time your blood group makes no difference to you at all. However, doctors may need to know your blood group before you have an operation. They can find this out by doing a simple blood test to see which of the chemicals A and B your blood contains.

Another important blood group is the rhesus group. This was first discovered in rhesus monkeys. People whose blood contains a chemical called rhesus factor are

The rhesus factor was discovered in rhesus monkeys like this.

blood group rhesus positive (Rh+). Those whose blood does not contain the rhesus factor are blood group rhesus negative (Rh-).

ABO and rhesus blood groups are usually referred to together. For example, someone might say they are "AB+", meaning their ABO group is AB and they are Rh+.

Giving blood from a Rh- person to a Rh+ person causes no problems, but giving Rh+ blood to a Rh- person can make them very ill. If a Rh+ mother is expecting a Rh- baby, her blood can harm the baby. Doctors can now check this before the baby is born and give the mother an injection to prevent any problems for the baby.

Giving Blood

A constant supply of blood is needed because there is a never-ending list of people who need blood transfusions. Doctors like to have a supply of blood available to replace any blood that might be lost during a major operation. Also, people who suffer serious accidents may need blood to replace what they have lost. Patients with some illnesses, such as leukaemia and anaemia, may also need to be given blood. Doctors can never know how many people will need blood, or when they will need it, so it is safest to make sure there is always plenty available.

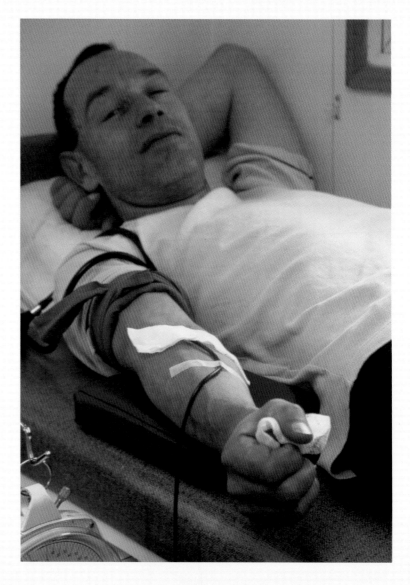

Giving blood is safe and may help to save another person's life.

Not everybody is allowed to give blood. Different countries have different rules, but in most countries you have to be over a minimum age. Until you are fully grown, it might harm your body if you give blood. Some countries also have an upper age limit.

To give blood, people go to a blood donation centre. Some are part of a hospital, but others are in mobile units like large caravans. Mobile units travel around so that it is as easy as possible for people to get to them and give blood.

Before a person gives blood, they are asked lots of questions and a small sample of their blood is tested. This is to check that it is safe for that person to give their blood.

Donated blood is often stored in large refrigerators like this one.

When everything is ready, the donor sits or lies on a special chair or bed. A sterile needle is put into a vein at the inside of their elbow, and a collecting bag is attached to the other end of the needle via a plastic tube. Blood flows out of the vein, down the tube and into the bag. When enough has been collected, the donor rests quietly for a while and then leaves.

Blood is stored at "blood banks". Donated blood may be refrigerated and stored as whole blood. It is often separated, though, and red blood cells, white blood cells, platelets and plasma are each stored separately. This means that blood is used efficiently – one patient may need plasma and another red blood cells, for example, so one blood donation can be used to treat more than one person.

Case notes

How do we know donated blood is safe?

Whenever a person gives blood, their blood is tested to find out which group it is. It is also tested to make sure that it does not contain any viruses or anything else that might harm a patient to whom the blood is given. As scientists discover more about diseases, they are able to carry out more advanced tests to check the donated blood is safe.

Blood Problems

Most people have healthy blood that does not cause them many problems. There are some blood disorders, though, that can cause serious problems for people.

Haemophilia This is an inherited condition, much more common in males than females, that prevents the blood from clotting properly. People with haemophilia bruise very easily and it is very difficult to stop the bleeding if they have a cut. In very bad cases, blood may leak into a child's joints, stopping them from forming properly and making them very painful. Until recently, doctors had no way of treating haemophilia. Now, though, it can be treated by regular injections of blood-clotting chemicals.

Sickle cell anaemia In this inherited disease, red blood cells lose their usual rounded shape and become stretched and twisted. These deformed red blood cells cannot carry as much oxygen as normal red blood cells, so the person feels tired and weak. These cells can also block blood vessels, causing pain, especially in joints and bones. Sickle cell anaemia can often be

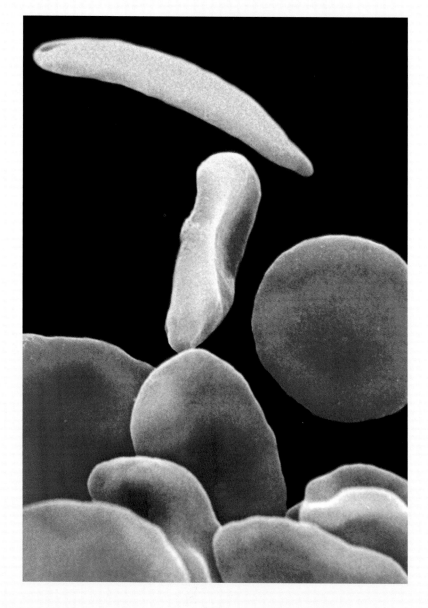

In sickle cell anaemia, red blood cells become deformed and twisted.

treated by medicines. Sometimes a blood transfusion is needed to provide extra healthy red blood cells.

Sickle cell anaemia, and a milder form known as sickle cell trait, are common in countries around the equator. Malaria, a disease carried by mosquitoes, is also common in these places. Scientists have found that having sickled blood cells makes the blood poisonous to these mosquitoes – so it protects you against malaria!

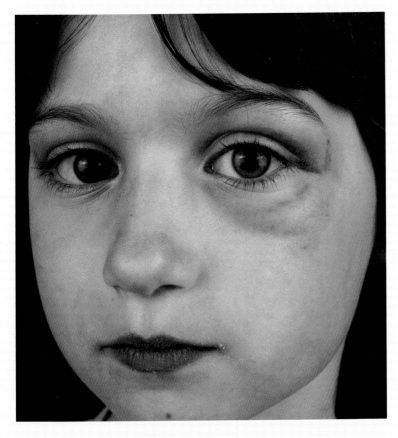

Bruises can be sore but they soon heal.

Leukaemia People with leukaemia have too many white blood cells in their blood. This means that none of the white blood cells can develop and work properly, so the body cannot defend itself against infections. The extra white blood cells also stop the bone marrow from making red blood cells, so oxygen transport is affected, making the person feel tired and weak. Leukaemia can be treated with special medicines (chemotherapy) and radiation (radiotherapy). Some patients may also receive a bone marrow transplant, often from a brother or sister.

Case notes

What is a bruise?

A bruise is usually the result of a knock or blow to the skin. This damages blood vessels in the skin, and blood leaks out of them. The surface of the skin is not damaged and so the blood cannot escape. Instead, it spreads out inside the skin and you see a dark mark – a bruise. This often has a dark, purply-blue colour to start with. After a few days, the colour fades to yellowy green as the body breaks up the blood cells and clears them away. Eventually, the bruise vanishes completely.

Glossary

aorta — The main artery carrying blood away from the heart.

artery — One of the large blood vessels carrying blood away from the heart.

atrium — One of the upper chambers of the heart.

bacteria — A type of micro-organism.

capillary — One of the tiniest blood vessels.

carbon dioxide — A waste gas produced by the body.

cardiac — To do with the heart.

circulation — The movement of blood around the body.

coronary — To do with the heart.

digestive system — Organs that break up and absorb your food.

germ — A micro-organism that can cause illness.

inherited — Passed on from one generation to the next.

kidneys — Organs that remove waste salts and water from the blood.

liver — The organ that controls many chemical reactions in the body.

nutrients — The parts of your food that your body can use.

oxygen — A gas that every part of your body needs in order to stay alive.

pericardium — The outer covering of the heart.

plasma — The liquid part of the blood.

platelet — A tiny cell fragment that helps blood to clot.

pulmonary — To do with the lungs.

red blood cell — The part of the blood that carries oxygen.

ribcage — Bones that form the chest and protect the heart and lungs.

septum — The central wall separating the two sides of the heart.

valve — A flap that controls the direction of blood flow.

vein — One of the large blood vessels that carry blood back to the heart.

vena cava — The main vein that carries blood back to the heart.

ventricle — One of the lower chambers of the heart.

virus — A micro-organism that can cause illness.

white blood cell — The part of the blood that protects you from illness and infection.

Further Information

Books

DK Guide to the Human Body
(Dorling Kindersley, 2004)

My Healthy Body: Blood and Heart
by Jen Green (Franklin Watts, 2003)

The Oxford Children's A to Z of the Human Body
by Bridget and Neil Ardley
(Oxford University Press, 2003)

Under the Microscope: Heart
by C. Gregory (Franklin Watts, 2001)

Usborne Internet-Linked Complete Book of the Human Body
by Anna Claybourne
(Usborne Publishing, 2003)

Websites

www.heartfoundation.com.au
click on "for kids"

www.bhf.org.uk
click on "young people" and then on "cbhf"

www.sciencemuseum.org.uk/imax/HumanBody

Index

Page numbers in **bold** refer to illustrations.